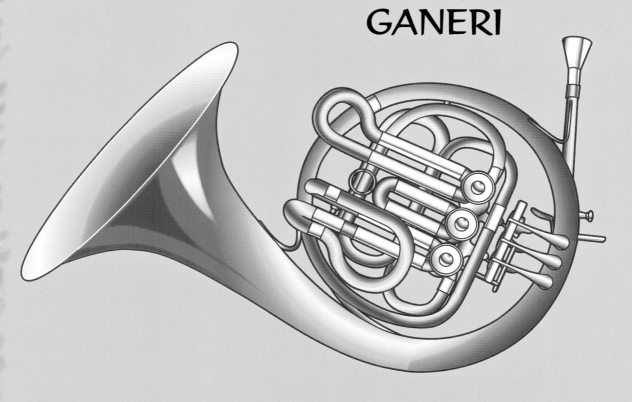

HOW THE WORLD MAKES MUSIC

BRASS INSTRUMENTS

ANITA GANERI

W

FRANKLIN WATTS

LONDON•SYDNEY

3579043

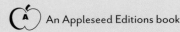 An Appleseed Editions book

First published in 2011 by Franklin Watts
338 Euston Road, London NW1 3BH

Franklin Watts Australia
Hachette Children's Books
Level 17/207 Kent St, Sydney, NSW 2000

© 2011 Appleseed Editions

Created by Appleseed Editions Ltd,
Well House, Friars Hill, Guestling,
East Sussex TN35 4ET

Designed by Guy Callaby
Illustrated by Graham Rosewarne
Edited by Jinny Johnson
Picture research by Su Alexander

ISBN 978-1-4451-0354-9

Dewey Classification: 788.9

A CIP catalogue for this book is available from the British Library.

Picture credits
l = left, r = right, t = top, b = bottom, c = centre
Title page l D D Coral/Shutterstock, cl Aruna Bhat/Alamy, cr Dusko/Shutterstock, r LM & APL/
Alamy; Contents page SandiMako/Shutterstock; P4 Lebrecht Music and Arts Photo Library/
Alamy; 5 Katrina Brown/Shutterstock; 6 Sandro Vannini/Corbis; 7 David Lyons/Alamy; 8 Buzz
Pictures/Alamy; 9 Dusko/Shutterstock; 10 Andrew Holt/Alamy; 11 Aruna Bhat/Alamy; 12 D D
Coral/Shutterstock; 13 Pictorial Press Ltd/Alamy; 14 PhotoStock-Israel/Alamy; 15 Horatiu Bota/
Shutterstock; 16 Israel Images/Alamy; 17 Anders Ryman/Alamy; 18 The British Museum; 19 Rolf
Richardson/Alamy; 20 INTERFOTO/Alamy; 21 SandiMako/Shutterstock; 23 Lebrecht Music and
Arts Photo Library/Alamy; 24 Albert H Teich/Shutterstock; 25 Jose Gil/Shutterstock;
27l Lebrecht Music and Arts Photo Library/Alamy, b Clive Chilvers/Shutterstock; 28 Lebrecht
Music and Arts Photo Library; 29 Kate Mount/Lebrecht Music and Arts Photo Library

Front cover: main image Jose Gil/Shutterstock; background image Oleksii Ambramov/
Shutterstock; top row (left to right) Sergey Kamshylin/Shutterstock; Clive Chilvers/Shutterstock;
SandiMako/Shutterstock; Dusko/Shutterstock

Printed in Singapore

Franklin Watts is a division of Hachette Children's Books,
an Hachette UK company.
www.hachette.co.uk

Contents

Brass instruments

People all over the world make music. They play musical instruments and sing songs when they are happy or sad, and as part of festivals and other ceremonies. People enjoy listening to music as they go about their daily lives.

The brass section of an orchestra, playing in a concert. The section includes trumpets, trombones, tubas and horns.

Origins

Modern brass instruments are made from metal. This is how they get their name. But they have their origins in many instruments made from lots of different materials, including shell, horn and hollow branches. What all these instruments have in common is that the player uses his or her lips to produce the sound.

Musical Notes

To sound any kind of brass instrument, the player presses both lips tightly against one end of a tube. As the player blows, his lips vibrate. It is these movements that set the air inside the instrument vibrating and produce sounds.

Ancient trumpets

People were playing very simple trumpets at least 3,500 years ago. In 1922, the tomb of Tutankhamun was discovered in Egypt. Tutankhamun was a pharaoh (king) of Ancient Egypt who died in around 1323 BCE. His tomb contained everything he needed for life after death, including a pair of trumpets. One trumpet was made from silver, the other from copper.

Musical Notes

In 1939, a trumpeter was allowed to play Tutankhamun's silver trumpet. A recording was made of the sound. Sadly, the force of the trumpeter's breath shattered the ancient instrument! (It has since been put back together again.)

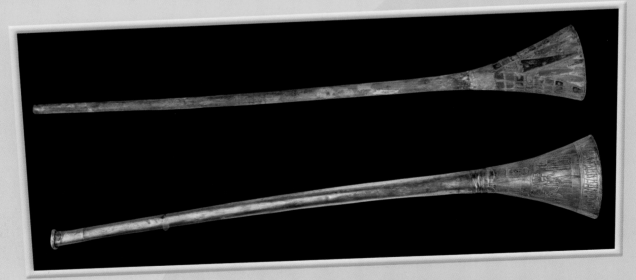

The two ancient trumpets found in Tutankhamun's tomb. They may have been used to send signals during battles.

War trumpets

The noise of trumpets was used in ancient times by armies to frighten their enemies. One of these war trumpets was the carynx, played by the Celts. This metal instrument was topped with an open-mouthed animal head to make it even more alarming.

This is a modern version of a carynx.

Large trumpets

The didgeridoo is a type of large trumpet that is played by the Aboriginal people of Australia. It is made from the hollowed-out branch of an eucalyptus tree. Traditionally, the branches were buried in the ground and left to be hollowed out by termites.

Musical Notes

The didgeridoo is played by blowing hard through vibrating lips. As the player squeezes air from his mouth down the tube, he also breathes in through his nose. This is called circular breathing. It allows the player to keep the sound going continuously.

Alphorns were originally used to send messages across the long distances in the mountains.

Alphorn

The alphorn is a gigantic instrument that is traditionally played in the mountains of Switzerland. It is carved out of wood and can measure up to 5 metres long.

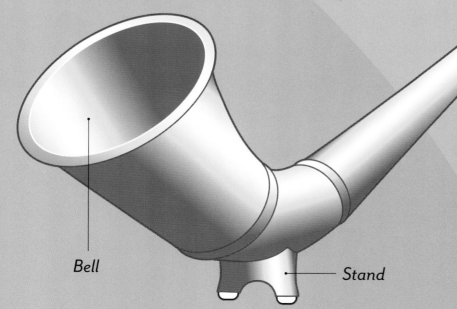

Mouthpiece

Bell

Stand

Sounding signals

Trumpets have been used throughout history to send signals. Players could only produce a few notes on simple trumpets, but the sound was loud and clear. In ancient Peru, the Moche people made trumpets out of clay. Other trumpets were made from bone, bark and wood.

A young boy plays a trumpet made from animal horn in Ethiopia, Africa. The sound of this trumpet can carry over a long distance.

Dung-chen

The dung-chen is a Tibetan trumpet. It is made out of brass or copper. It can be up to 3 metres long, but it is built in sections that collapse to make it shorter for storage.

Bell

Mouthpiece

Dung-chen are usually played in pairs. They are linked with the Buddhist religion. Their sound signals the start of important rituals, as well as dawn and sunset.

Musical Notes

The dung-chen produces a very, very low sound. When two of these instruments are played together in the high mountain valleys of Tibet, the echoing noise can be quite eerie.

Orchestral trumpet

The orchestral trumpet has a bright and brilliant sound. It can be clearly heard even when the whole orchestra is playing. This type of trumpet is also played in military and jazz bands.

The members of a military band have to learn to play their instruments while they are marching. Military bands also include some wind and percussion instruments.

Changing note

A trumpet player makes some notes by changing the shape made by her lips. The orchestral trumpet also has three valves. These allow the player to make other notes. When the player presses down one of the valves, it connects to an extra set of tubing. This means the vibrating air has further to travel, and the note sounded is lower.

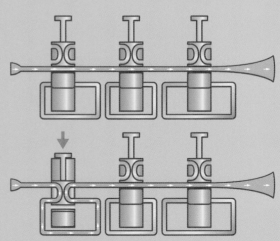

Musical Notes

The trumpet is often played in jazz music. Louis Armstrong was one of the most famous jazz trumpeters. He came from New Orleans in the USA. His nickname was Satchmo (short for Satchelmouth) because of his wide mouth and big grin.

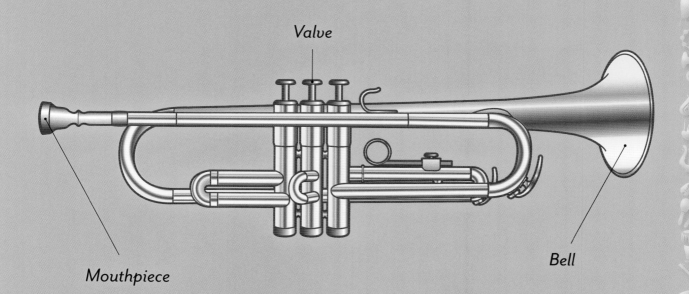

Valve

Mouthpiece

Bell

Trombone

The trombone has a deeper and richer sound than the trumpet. It also has an unusual way of producing different notes. The trombone player makes some notes by changing the shape of his lips. But other notes are made by moving a piece of tubing in and out of the instrument. This tubing is called a slide.

A person who plays a trombone is called a trombonist or trombone player. Trombones are played in many different kinds of music, from classical to folk and pop.

The slide

The trombone slide is a U-shaped tube with a crossbar. The player holds the crossbar with his right hand to move the slide in and out. With the slide pushed right out, the length of tubing is much greater than with the slide pulled back in. The further the vibrating air has to travel through the tube, the deeper the note.

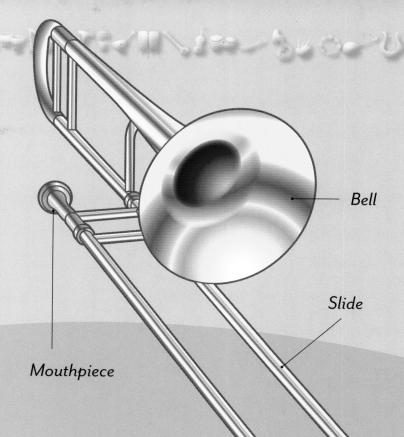

Bell

Slide

Mouthpiece

Musical Notes

Brass players can use devices called mutes to alter the sound of their instruments.

A mute fits snugly into the end of the instrument and makes the sound quieter. Different mutes also have different effects on the sound. Some mutes give a more piercing noise; others make a buzzing sound.

Mute

Ancient horns

In ancient times, people made musical instruments from the horns of animals, such as cows and sheep. They simply cut a small hole in the end of the horn, then blew down the horn to produce a sound. In Africa, people often cut a hole into the side of the horn. They blew across this hole to produce a sound.

A man blowing a shofar. In ancient times, it was blown to announce important events, such as the arrival of the king.

Shofar

The shofar is a special horn used in the Jewish religion. It is usually made from the horn of a ram. It is still played on important days in the Jewish religious calendar, such as Rosh Hashanah (the Jewish New Year) and Yom Kippur (the Day of Atonement).

Mouthpiece

Musical Notes

Some ancient horns are not made from horn at all. Simple horns were made from clay and wood, large shells, and even out of armadillo tails! This boy is blowing a large shell of a conch, a kind of sea creature, which gives a low, deep sound.

Ivory horns

In medieval times, some horns were carved out of elephant ivory. Only very wealthy people could afford such luxurious horns. These ivory horns were called oliphants.

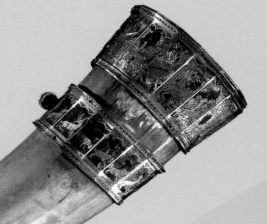

The Savernake Horn

Ivory horns were carried by nobles to sound signals when they were out hunting. This hunting horn gets its name from the Savernake Forest in Wiltshire, England. It was made in the 1300s, and it is decorated with silver bands.

The Savernake Horn is made from ivory and decorated with silver. It is engraved with animals, including a lion and a unicorn. The horn was last blown in 1940.

Musical Notes

The name 'oliphant' comes from an ancient word for elephant. The ivory used to make oliphants usually came from elephants.

Lur

Some of these ancient musical instruments can still be played today. The sounds of the lur are heard on several CDs that have been made by Scandinavian brass players.

A lur is an ancient Scandinavian horn, made from bronze. It has a long curved tube, topped by a flat disc. Many of these instruments have been dug out of boggy ground in Denmark and other parts of southern Scandinavia. Lurs were usually played in pairs.

A pair of lur blowers. A lur was around 2 metres long. It has a long, curved handle to make it easier to carry. The lur was probably sounded in battles to frighten the enemy and send signals to troops.

Bugle

The bugle is a simple metal horn that has no valves. The bugle player sounds different notes by changing the shape of her lips. This means that bugles can play only a few notes.

Since the 18th century, armies have used bugles to send signals. Different patterns of notes, or 'calls', sent different messages to the soldiers on the battlefield.

Mouthpiece

Bell

Bugle calls

There were many different bugle calls and each had its own meaning. For example, one call was sounded to tell the soldiers to 'go forward'. Another meant 'cease fire'. Bugle calls were also used in camp to tell soldiers when to wake up, or to signal meal times.

Musical Notes

At military funerals, and at ceremonies to remember those who have died in battle, a bugler plays a famous call, known as the 'Last Post'. This call was originally used to signal the end of the day to soldiers in camp.

Orchestral horn

The horn that is played in the Western orchestra is often called the French horn. The French horn has lots of loops and coils of tubing which end in a wide opening, called the bell. The player holds the horn by placing his right hand inside the bell.

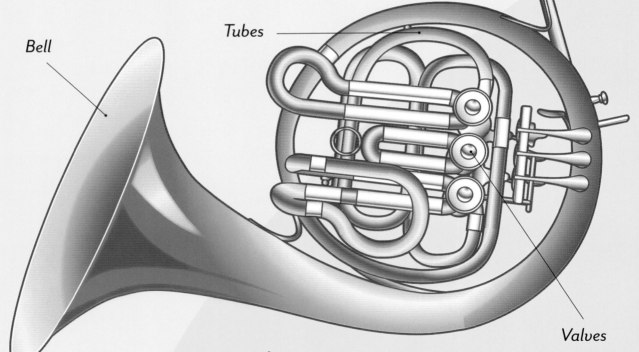

Mouthpiece

Tubes

Bell

Valves

Most French horns are double horns but some are single horns.

Two in one

The French horn is, in fact, two horns in one. One set of tubes plays lower notes; another set plays higher, brighter notes. The player uses valves to switch between the two sets of tubing.

Learning to play the French horn takes lots of practice! Players need to get their fingering, blowing and breathing technique right so that they can make a smooth sound.

Musical Notes

There are usually four horns in an orchestra. But when a German composer called Richard Strauss wrote his Alpine Symphony, he included parts for 20 horns! (His father was a horn player.)

Tuba

The brass section of an orchestra is made up of trumpets, trombones, French horns and tubas. The tuba is the biggest instrument, and it makes the deepest sounds. Tubas are also played in military bands.

Tuba players in a military band. Tubas are also played in jazz, classical and big band music where a booming sound is needed.

Sitting and marching

In an orchestra, the tuba player sits on a chair and rests the instrument on his lap. But for marching, the tuba is rested on the player's shoulder. The bell points forwards rather than upwards.

Mouthpipe

Bell

Valve tube

Valves

Musical Notes

The sousaphone is named after an American bandmaster, called John Philip Sousa. It is a kind of tuba that fits around the body of the player with the bell pointing forwards above the player's head. It is very popular in marching bands.

Band instruments

Marching bands and brass bands have many different types of brass instruments. In British brass bands, the instrument that often plays the tunes is the cornet. The cornet is like a trumpet, but it is shorter and has a softer sound. Cornets are also played in marching bands.

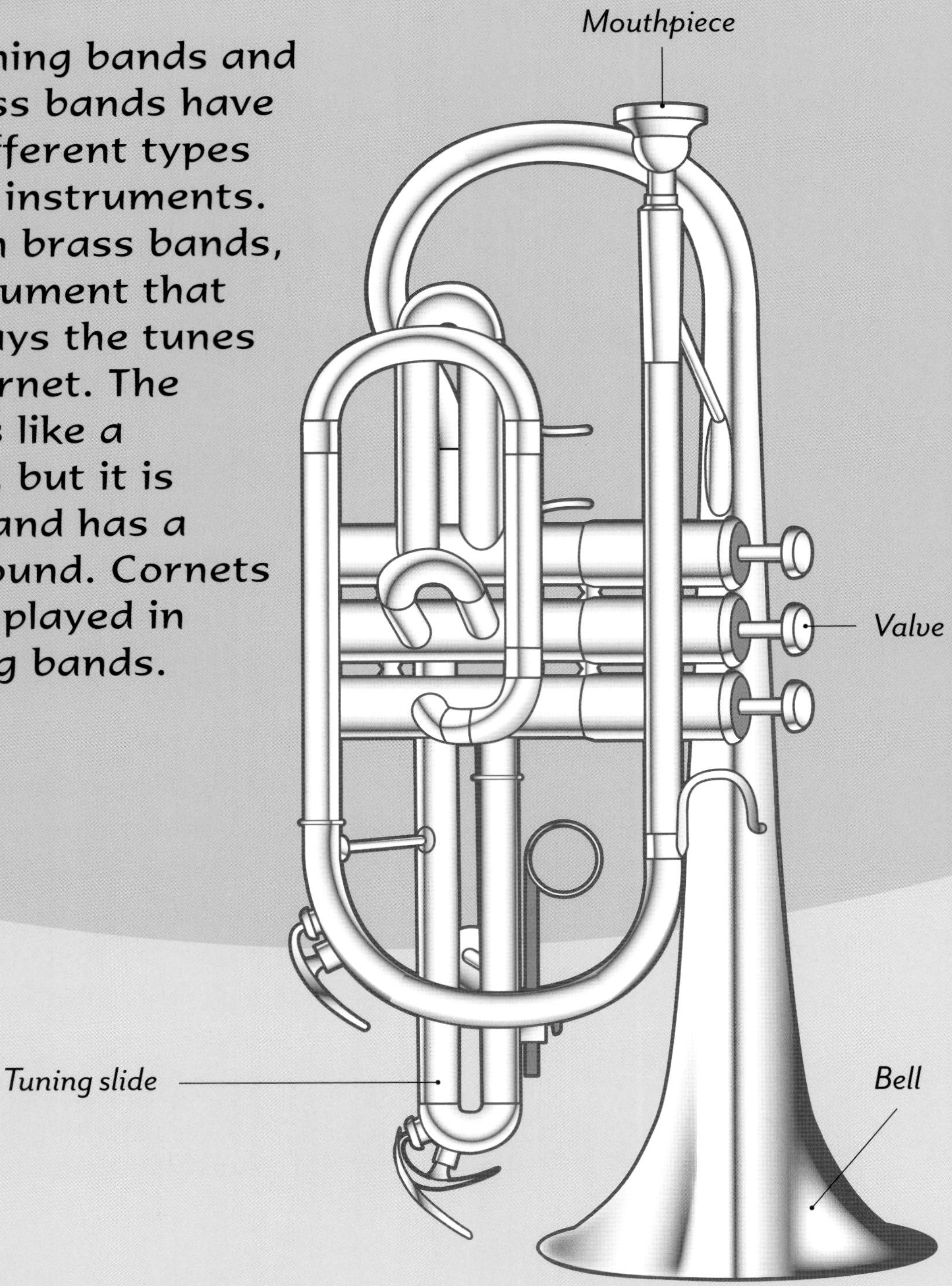

Mouthpiece

Valve

Tuning slide

Bell

Flugelhorn and euphonium

The flugelhorn is like a cornet, but it has a wider tube and bigger bell. This means that it makes a darker sound than the cornet. The euphonium is popular in brass bands and marching bands. It is like a small tuba, and it has a rich, velvety sound.

The euphonium can be played as part of an orchestra, or as a solo instrument. Many euphonium players play other brass instruments too, such as trumpets.

Musical Notes

Other brass instruments played in bands include alto horns, mellophones, tenor trombones and baritone horns. Some bands also feature a percussion section and sometimes wind instruments.

Serpent

The serpent is a strange instrument that is a cross between a brass and a wind instrument. With its winding shape, it certainly lives up to its name. It was invented in France in the 1590s.

This serpent was made in about 1820 from pearwood, leather, brass and ivory.

Wooden snake

The serpent's curved body is made from wood, with six fingerholes in two groups of three. It has a metal mouthpiece, rather like that of a trombone. In the 1600s and 1700s, the serpent was played in churches, and then it became popular in military bands. It was eventually replaced by instruments such as the tuba and the euphonium.

Musical Notes

The serpent had a cousin called the ophicleide. This instrument was developed in the 1800s. Unlike the serpent, it was made from metal, and it had keys rather than fingerholes. Its name combines the Greek words for 'serpent' and 'key'.

Words to remember

Aboriginal
The Aboriginals were the first people to live in Australia, many thousands of years ago.

bell
In a brass instrument, the bell is the bell-shaped end of the tube.

brass
A metal that is a mixture of two other metals – copper and zinc.

Buddhist
A person who follows the teaching of the Buddha, a holy man who lived in India thousands of years ago.

Celts
People who lived in Britain, France and Spain before the Romans.

clay
Soft earth or mud that is moulded into shape, then baked hard.

copper
A reddish-brown metal.

horn
Animal horn was once used to make many objects, including musical instruments.

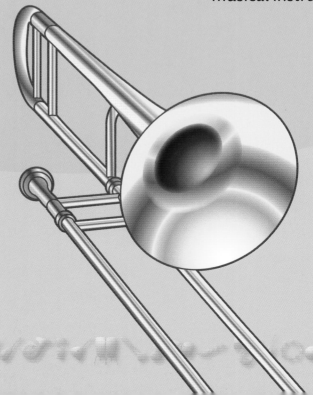

ivory
The material that an elephant's tusks are made from.

marching band
A band that marches as it plays, in time to the music.

mouthpiece
In a brass instrument, the mouthpiece is the end of the tube that a player blows down.

mute
A device placed in the bell of a brass instrument to make the sound quieter.

percussion instruments
Musical instruments, such as drums, cymbals and tambourines.

pharaoh
In Ancient Egypt, the title given to the ruler.

slide
A piece of tubing on a trombone.

termites
Termites are tiny, ant-like creatures.

valve
In a brass instrument, a device that a player presses to alter the length of the tube and the sound of the note.

vibrations
When something, such as air, moves backwards and forwards very quickly.

wind instruments
Musical instruments, such as flutes, clarinets and oboes.

Index

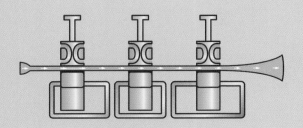